Anne Effelsberg

FLOWER ARRANGING

AN ILLUSTRATED GUIDE

TRANSEDITION
BOOKS

CONTENTS

INTRODUCTION

Flowers are absolutely fascinating. They come in an endless variety of forms: with large and small petals in a multiplicity of shapes and variety of textures – soft and hard, rough and smooth; with a delicate or strong fragrance; with thick or thin stems and with or without leaves. The unique quality of each flower or plant and the particular effect it produces, is due to many different factors including the contour of flower and leaf, the interplay of texture, surface and color and the graceful lines drawn by stems that vary in thickness, straightness and flexibility. The myriad visual forms which nature takes are a constant wonder! The unique quality of a flower is also influenced by its environment, the climate, and its natural habitat: a shady or an exposed location, a garden, a meadow, woodland, pond or lakeside. Certain visual impressions are an instant reminder of time and place: oxeye daisies can make us think of meadows and summertime and wild anemones can remind us of woodlands and springtime.

Once, when I was a child, I well remember walking miles to pick some wild anemones, only to find that by the time I got home they had all wilted. These delicate and sensitive flowers remained etched on my memory and the longing to see them in my home grew ever stronger. My frequent attempts to gather such flowers successfully having failed, I finally had the idea of taking a plastic bag and some wet cotton wool with me and at last managed to pick a small bunch which I succeeded in displaying at home. As well as being able to enjoy these delicate blooms, I had learned a valuable lesson: cut flowers are not some dead material, they have to be cared for if we want them to survive for any length of time.

This memory is vivid and so is the picture of the cornfield around whose edge I used to pick colorful posies of wild flowers. Their blaze of rich color gave me a deeply satisfying, happy feeling. Ultimately it is such experiences that influence how we treat flowers in later life: a legacy of wonder, joy and affection, an ever-increasing awareness of differences of detail and the ability to distinguish what is typical in a plant and what is exceptional.

I have also always been impressed by the process of creation: the fascination of nature's stages of development, from propagation, seedling, through full-flowering magnificence to gradual decay. All this can be observed in a single flower as effectively as in the seasons. We often walk past things in life without really seeing them — including flowers. But the close, detailed, and deliberate observation of an individual flower is necessary if we are to be fully aware of its individuality in an arrangement. If you take the time to examine carefully a common flower, like an iris for example, you will discover its particular features: the position and number of petals; the numerous triangular shapes produced by their juxtaposition; the bright yellow "flight paths" to guide insects, the shape of bud and blossom and the shining or matt surface of leaf and flower. There is so much to discover and wonder at.

When I am choosing a flower for an arrangement, the first thing I do is to look at it closely in detail. It is useful, too, to be aware of some fundamental points when working with flowers and the following section, on the principles of flower arranging, gives basic information applicable to all kinds of arrangements from a bunch of flowers to a formal bowl.

MATERIALS, TECHNIQUES AND THE

PRINCIPLES OF FLOWER ARRANGING

What do we need to know when working with flowers? The answer falls into three categories: the basic manual skills (for instance, how to wire flowers, bind a wreath together, cut stems correctly); an understanding of material (which flowers and foliage will achieve the effect you want); knowledge of the mechanics (the equipment used to hold the arrangements firmly in place) and containers (which are best for the various kinds of arrangements).

And then there is also the whole question of the creative aspect – the artistic element – that is so enriched by working with flowers. In this respect, close observation of the plant material being used is as important in influencing the result as the choice of flowers, containers or location of the arrangement.

But above all, let your imagination and self-expression be your inspiration.

MATERIALS

Tools

from left to right:
- Pruning shears for cutting flowers, small branches and twigs
- Sharp flower knife
- Scissors for cutting raffia, tape
- Pliers for cutting wire

Binding materials

from left to right:
- Natural raffia, which should be soaked in water before use to soften and prevent tearing
- Florist's binding tape: useful for tying bunches of flowers together
- String in two colors for use where ties remain visible
- Colored raffia for use where ties remain visible
- Green raffia for use with bouquets in a container

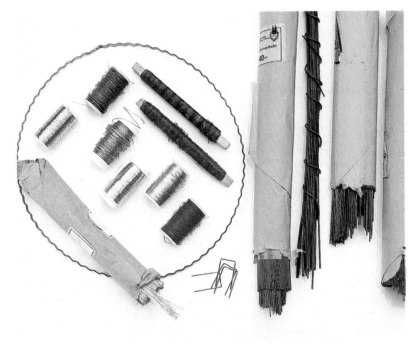

Wire

from left to right:
• Wire ring for small wreaths
• Thin silver wire for tying fine, light material
• Colored wire for use in affixing items around containers or for visible binding: for example, covering a container with moss. *Note*: plain wire will rust
• Wire wound around sticks: useful when tying wreaths
• Staples to anchor flat material
• Wire in differing lengths and thicknesses for use with heavier materials

Essential mechanics

top, from left to right:
• Nylon thread
• Plastic pinholder, used with fixing strip and floral tape to anchor floral foam to flat surfaces
• Floral tape and fixing strip

middle:
• Single stem holders, plain and covered
• Plant spray
• Floral foam: this is cut and sculpted to size and soaked in water before use
• Decorative crepe paper, available in a variety of colors

Roots, stumps and branches all fulfill a dual purpose: they are visually attractive and they offer structural support to an arrangement. A lattice of twigs wedged into a container provides a simple foundation. Branches which have a number of offshoots growing from the same point are also useful.

Pebbles, shells and marbles look very attractive in glass containers which show them off to their best advantage.

Wire netting comes in different mesh sizes and the coated kind does not rust. It can be used flat or crushed into a ball but should always be invisible in the arrangement. A combination of wire and pebbles can make a good support for larger stems and branches.

Floral foam must first be cut to size and shape and then soaked thoroughly in water for some time. When wedging floral foam into the container, remember to leave a few gaps so that

water can be added easily.

To anchor floral foam to a flat dish, a plastic pinholder must first be stuck down with fixing strip and the foam pressed onto it (see page 11). The disadvantage of this is that when the time comes to change the arrangement the adhesive can only be completely removed with a solvent. Leaves, sand, gravel and similar materials make a good covering for this kind of base. However, certain flowers like narcissi, anemones, cyclamens and Christmas roses, which have really soft and sappy stems, will not last any time in floral foam. A pinholder or crushed wire netting is the best support for this type of stem.

The highly practical metal pinholder comes in varying shapes and sizes. For home use it is ideal, as it gives support and stability and can be used over and over again. But it is not suitable for arrangements which are to be transported from one place to another

Covering containers

From left to right on page 10:
• Simple earthenware pot partially covered with moss (also effective when completely covered)
• Moss covered vase. Colored wire adds to the artistic effect
• Shallow plant bowl covered in hay, bound with contrasting colored raffia. Containers may be covered in a similar fashion using leaves, ferns or ornamental grasses to even greater effect

Containers and mechanics

Top row, from left to right
• Pail with wire netting cover, placed in a basket
• Shallow bowl containing floral foam, anchored and covered in sand
• Seashells heaped in a bowl

Bottom row, from left to right
• Lattice support made of twigs and wedged into a small bowl
• Metal pinholder in a dish
• Marbles in a glass container
• Plastic pinholder pressed into fixing strip ready for floral foam to be firmly affixed

BASIC TECHNIQUES

unless it has been secured very firmly. Flower stems should be cut straight across and branches cut at an angle.

Single stem holders are extremely useful for arrangements where only a few flowers need to be in water. As a rule you should first fill the holder with water and then place the cut stem in it. Stem holders will almost certainly need topping up very regularly.

There are times when wiring different plant materials is very helpful in certain arrangements. Wire pushed gently up inside a stem allows it to be bent at a particular angle, for example, in a bridal bouquet, or it can be used to lengthen the stems of dried flowers. In

the following pages you will find ideas for using wire in different ways: tying a bow, lengthening a stem or securing stem holders. When buying florist's wire, make sure a qualified person advises you – if the wire is too thick the stem will break and if it is too thin the necessary support will be lacking. *Tip*: When twisting a support wire around a stem (see page 13), hold the wire at the very end to help you wind it securely. These and other basic techniques take some experimentation to perfect but mastering them will make every difference to your arrangements and are well worth the time you spend.

Tying and wiring a bow

First make a loop in the ribbon, with the short end hanging down on the left (*top left*). Hold in position with one hand and, with the other hand, make a second loop from the longer piece of ribbon (*top right*). Press the center of the bow firmly together and hold in one hand. Take a piece of wire with the end hooked over and secure the bow by twisting the long end of the wire around the bow and short end (*bottom left and right*).

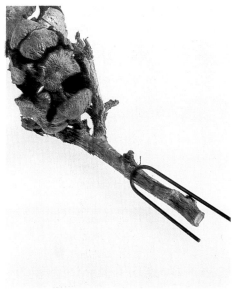

Wiring stems

The wire is bent over at one end and hooked round the stem. It is held in position with one hand while the long end of the wire is twisted around both the stem and the short end. This may also be done leaving the ends of wire the same length. If the wire is pointed at one end, it is useful to leave that end longer and use it to push the stem into place in the arrangement. The thickness of wire you need to use will depend on the stability, length and weight of stem to be wired.

Stem holders

Single stem holders, which are available from florists or specialist shops, are first filled with water (left) and then covered, either in moss or plastic tape. The stem holder is secured in the arrangement with wire and the top fits so tightly that water cannot leak out, even when it is positioned horizontally. However, the flower stem must exactly fit the hole in the cap to prevent leakage.

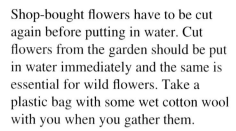

CUT FLOWERS

Care of cut flowers

Here are a few tips for looking after cut flowers:

• Buy only flowers that look really fresh and are in good condition.

• Remember that at certain times, like Easter or Christmas, flowers may be more expensive so check the quality very closely.

• Untrimmed, soft stems and dirty water indicate lack of care and are signs that flowers have stood in the same water for some time.

• Flowers grown out of season may exhibit qualities untypical of their species like soft stems and limp leaves

• In cold weather avoid buying flowers that are mainly in bud as they are unlikely to bloom.

• Flowers bought in bloom in season show their quality and usually keep longer than those out of season.

• Some flowers from the garden are ready for cutting when their buds show color (for instance hyacinths, lilies, tulips, narcissi and gladioli) and some when they are in full bloom (like larkspurs, carnations, daisies, snapdragons and cornflowers). Roses are ready for cutting when the sepals bend downward.

• Never cut flowers in the heat of midday or in a strong wind.

• Leaves and shoots are inclined to wilt quickly, which is why flowers should be put in water as soon as possible.

Shop-bought flowers have to be cut again before putting in water. Cut flowers from the garden should be put in water immediately and the same is essential for wild flowers. Take a plastic bag with some wet cotton wool with you when you gather them.

• The life of your cut flowers can be extended by being wrapped tightly in paper, put in lukewarm water and left to stand overnight in a cool dry place.

• For best results flowers should be put in water that has been boiled or has stood for twelve hours.

• To slow down decay, all leaves on the lower third of a stem should be removed. Removing a few leaves from the top of the stem will also help reduce dehydration.

• Any flowers which show poor recovery from initial signs of wilting or decay should be cut very short.

• Generally speaking, stems should be cut at an angle using a sharp knife. Thicker stems should, however, be cut straight.

• The ends of twigs or branches which exude sap should be held in boiling water for a few seconds after cutting. Sunflowers, dahlias and chrysanthemums should also be conditioned in this way.

• Flowers last longer if stems are re-cut each day.

• Containers should be kept scrupulously clean to avoid the growth of bacteria.

• You can buy certain chemicals from your florist which will prolong the freshness of your flowers. Some are for specific species, some for general use. If you use these products, daily cutting and water changing becomes unnecessary. Always read the label on the product carefully and use the recommended quantities.

To tie a bunch of flowers

1. Prepare flowers by removing all the leaves on the lower third of the stem. These must be cut off cleanly with a sharp tool or the stem will rot. Grip the stem with the thumb, index and middle finger of one hand at precisely the point where the bunch is to be tied together. Stem should incline to the right.

2. Place the second flower over the first one. This should incline to the left. Press stems together with your thumb.

3 and 4. Subsequent flowers are inclined in the same direction as the second one but each one should be inclined a little further.

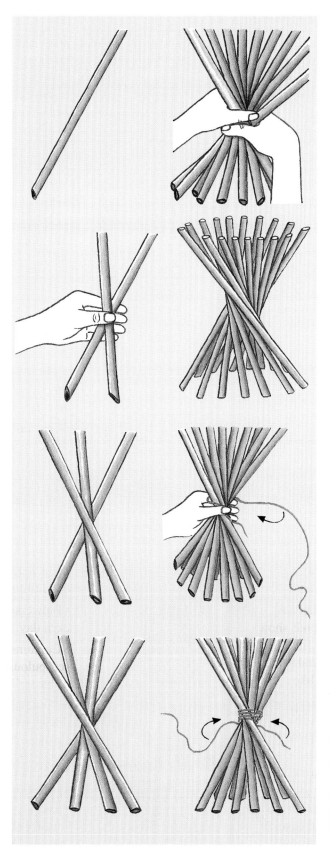

5. Continue adding flowers until bunch is the required size, turning it from time to time to achieve a symmetrical shape.

6. The result is a spiral but the stems should not cross.

7. Finally, hold the shorter end of a piece of raffia in place with your thumb and twist the longer end once around the stem.

8. Now, using your other hand, pull through the raffia you are holding down and twist it round the stems several times. The bunch may now be placed flat and a knot tied in the raffia. Finally, cut the ends level.

PLANNING YOUR ARRANGEMENT

When designing an arrangement for the home there are certain points that need to be considered:

Where the arrangement is going to be placed will often determine the shape of container and the type of flowers to be used. For example, a dinner table needs a flat arrangement so that guests can converse easily across the table. Having chosen the setting you now have to decide on the flowers, the color scheme and the outline and balance of the arrangement.

If you wish to create an arrangement for a particular container – a straight, tall glass vase for instance – you have to decide on the right place for it to stand, taking into account background and surroundings. Next comes the choice of flowers. Here you also have to consider the different ways of arranging the flowers: should they spill over and hang down, gracefully twining round the vase, or should you decide on a horizontal outline that will contrast with the vertical lines of the vase? Should you use a single, tall flower or will you perhaps decide on an arrangement that just peeps over the vase giving yet another effect?

If you wish to create an arrangement for a special occasion, then you have to ask yourself what kind of mood you want to create. Should the arrangement be soft and dainty, cool or romantic, dreamy, simple or formally elegant? Once this has been decided, you then have to consider which flowers will best achieve the effect you want. The choice of color scheme, container and mechanics then has to be made and, of course, the appropriate form that the

The setting

The container

Special occasions

final design is to take.

In summertime one might use sweet peas to express tenderness; marguerites, cornflowers, poppies and ornamental grasses to express happiness and a feeling of summer. Or a single water-lily leaf in a flat glass container might give an air of refreshing coolness.

Nature Natural settings, for example a grassy clearing, can form the inspiration for an arrangement. If this is the case, think about the overall impression you want to reflect in your design. Was it the myriad dots and patches of color that inspired you? If so, you would arrange your flowers loosely and at random so that the colors form their own kaleidoscope. Or was it the solid areas of color that attracted you? Then you would tie your bunches firmly together, segregating each patch of color. Or maybe your ideas were influenced by different kinds of grasses. Then you would choose the darker colors and take a narrow container with an elongated opening, a rectangular vase for instance, and with its shape you would arrange your flowers side by side, their serried ranks and crossed stems providing an important feature in your design. You might even place the arrangement in a position above eye level.

Perhaps a certain characteristic of nature left a great impression on you? The tendency, for instance, of plants to turn toward the light? This can be portrayed by arranging sunflowers (helianthus) of the same length in a line and bending the stems in the same direction; or you might arrange a trailing plant, like clematis, in such a way that it inclines sideways while ensuring the blossoms point upward. There are many ways to express characteristics observed in nature. If we wish to reproduce an emotion connected with a particular season, for instance the awakening and promise of spring, we can do so by tucking a few spring flowers into an arrangement of dried ones – to peer out from somber grasses. A nest, made out of trailing plants, in which a small, half-hidden bunch of flowers can be seen, is also delightful. These are just a few ways to suggest different impressions of nature. Have a look around for others when you are on a walk, especially when the seasons are changing.

And one single impression may be conveyed in a number of ways. Repetition can be used to good effect to give the impression of movement in a certain direction. Grass brushed all in one direction can suggest the effect of wind blowing over a field. Arranging plant material in a different fashion from the way it naturally grows can also be effective – for example, placing horse-chestnut tree "candles" so that the blossoms point downward instead of up. This emphasizes the fact that the individual tiny flowers in fact always point upward (see page 38).

If you decide to reproduce an impression from nature, it is best to stick to one or two features at a time. It is impossible to represent every aspect of nature in one arrangement – such impressions are influenced by so many elements: earth, sky, perspective, light, water and wind. An individual arrangement can express only a small part of this whole – which is why nature should not merely be copied. The more clearly and consistently a certain aspect is stressed, the clearer it will become to the observer, who will realize that the effect of your arrangement was achieved by design.

Details

One particular flower, twig or kind of grass forms the starting point of an arrangement. What is the best way to present a flower? By creating an arrangement that consists only of this one species or by arranging a variety of species together? Should the stems be left long or cut short? Should they be placed in the container vertically or at an angle? Which particular container do you wish to use and where is it going to be positioned? Should flowers of one variety be placed singly throughout the arrangement or should they be grouped together?

To highlight the individuality of a flower you may either arrange it with others of its own kind or you may mix it with other species. Either can be effective; the second method will emphasize the beauty created by the interaction of contours, flow of movement, and color. The impression that you are intending to produce may also lie in the blossom itself. In this case it would be right to cut the stems short so as not to distract the eye from the flower. Full-blown peonies, lilies, and certain carnations can look very attractive treated in this way. But there are flowers whose stems cannot be shortened radically as this would destroy their character – snapdragons for instance.

You may be particularly attracted by the distinctive shape of a flower stem which has grown in an unusual manner or by a contorted branch, and here you would then choose your container, color scheme and design to emphasize this characteristic. The movement of an undulating stem might be contrasted by the addition of still elements like simple, rounded buds, flat leaves or a very plain container.

However, perhaps it is the plant's texture that is interesting – the smooth and translucent surface of certain flowers; the velvety soft texture of some roses. These features can be highlighted by placing them next to contrasting textures like the hard and shining rose hip or the fleecy, soft traveler's joy. Take care, however, not to use too many different forms and colors as these can be merely distracting and you will lose the effect you want to achieve.

The color of a flower may also be highlighted in a number of ways. The effect may be strengthened by arranging circles of flowers of ever-lightening shades around a central deep-colored bloom. For example, you might start off with a red flower in the center and end with an outer circle of orange flowers. A bright orange flower may be highlighted by a cool complementary color, like a shade of blue or a subtle pink.

Variety

Sometimes you may want to create a large arrangement containing a wide variety of flowers and foliage of different seasons and origins (florist and garden flowers), just so that you can enjoy the whole glorious effect. In this case no emphasis is placed on any particular flower. It is the combination of different elements and their attractive symmetry, which creates the effect. In an arrangement that depends on a wide variety of flowers and foliage in differing sizes, and on the varied lines of movement created by numerous stems, textures, and colors, it is important to keep the outline simple and balanced.

Here, too, the principle applies that the clearer you are about the effect you want to produce, the more successful it will be. If your intention is to create a luxuriously warm, soft, and splendid effect, you should use such colors as muted reds, with a number of different shades of green, and trailing plants that twist softly around your container. One way to achieve such an effect would be to arrange lilies with dahlias or roses – combining flowers of differing origins and which bloom naturally in different seasons. It is the interaction between all these elements – impossible to put into words – which plays on the imagination and emotions.

Producing the effect you desire in an arrangement can only be successfully achieved by being aware of the typical, as well as the individual, characteristics of each flower – though the effect may be heightened by including such objects as candles and shells, and by using fruit and other plant materials to help create a visual atmosphere. However, do ensure the flowers are the dominant feature.

CREATING A PARTICULAR ATMOSPHERE

The Seasons

Many different effects can be created in your home with flower arrangements. You can bring the atmosphere of a particular season into the house by highlighting the effect of a certain seasonal flower.

While spring flowers, peeping out through trailing plants, create the promise of the gradual emergence of spring, a summer arrangement might be rich in color, form and variety of plants – celebrating the glory of nature at the peak of seasonal perfection.

Autumn is the season of nostalgia – a reminder of the past glories of spring and summer – while bridging the way to the dormant season of winter. Autumn can have the warmth of summer or the chill of winter. It is the season not only of ripeness and mellow reflection but also of gradual withdrawal. This is the time of year for those flowers with rounded forms and variety of textures, like chrysanthemums, which group so attractively together.

And then we come to silent, still, almost monochrome winter. Blooms no longer draw the eye – it is the contour and construction of leafless trees and shrubs, now undisguised by greenery, that attract our gaze. But although the landscape may appear dormant, out of our sight, nature prepares for spring. Simple, clear shapes, which highlight the coldness of winter, are now the keynote of beautiful arrangements. Or you may wish to hint at the coming of spring by using warmer colors in among varied plant material.

This is, of course, only a brief and subjective idea of the atmosphere of the seasons and there are many other moods and impressions which will be very personal to you. In my flower arranging, I try to reflect on such effects as light, weather and the time of day. A stroll in the rain, which was actually enjoyed, might prove the inspiration for a hearty, fun arrangement or, if it was not, might result in a soft, shrouded feel to a design. And, there are many sources of inspiration in addition to nature.

You might, for instance, wish to create a mood that is cheerful but restrained and unobtrusive at the same time and so you would choose small flowers in pastel shades that are mostly still in bud – like those used in the chapter on spring (see pages 34–35). Or you might wish to produce a simple, happy table arrangement – for a birthday table perhaps. For this I would choose

Emotions, moods and statements

simple garden flowers in a mixture of colors, like yellow, red, violet, and orange and keep the arrangement very natural looking. (See spring table decoration, page 30).

In contrast to a hot or hectic day, I like to see cool, tranquil arrangements which calm me down and are not too abundant or showy to be relaxing. This mood can be achieved by using only a few clear shapes and colors. The top illustration on page 41 is a perfect example of this: a single yellow lily and a little greenery arranged in a container covered with green moss. A warm, dreamy arrangement, a bouquet which appears to have been arranged by chance rather than design, can be achieved by arranging a few strands of hop shoots and ivy, picked out with fruit and chestnuts, in the manner of a painting.

I like to sketch out in my mind a picture with a particular atmosphere when arranging flowers for the dinner table or elsewhere in my home. While I know that everyone gets a slightly different impression from my work, arranging flowers over many years has taught me one thing: nobody ever says that a cool, clear design has given them an impression of warmth. Nor has anyone ever been upset by an arrangement containing a variety of colors – unless the colors clashed harshly. The statement you wish to make in an arrangement will be understood if you have taken care with your selection. When deciding the shape of an arrangement, it is helpful to use the intended effect as a starting point, especially for a dinner party or buffet table.

While flower arrangements can influence your feelings, it is equally possible to use them to express your own moods. Great care must be taken over the choice of every element of an arrangement in order to achieve a desired effect. This takes practice but using your intuition and self-expression can often achieve greater success than the programmed, text-book approach of some professional florists. It is, after all, your creation, unique to you.

The room Is the design intended to underline the atmosphere of a particular room? In this case, an effect appropriate to the surroundings might be chosen (for example, a classic arrangement in a formal room), or a complete contrast might be equally effective. For example, a stark, modern room might be attractively offset by a rich, flowing, full arrangement.

Immediate surroundings Consider the background and area where the arrangement is to stand. Does the texture of wall and shelf already create an attractive contrast to that of your flowers? Flowers and foliage can produce an entirely different effect when placed in front of a rough textured wall or a smooth wood surface. What effect will surrounding colors have on the whole arrangement?

Nearby objects What objects are situated near the arrangement? A painting? A mirror? A bowl of fruit? Is there any artistic link to be made between these objects and your arrangement? You might reflect their colors or make your design a similar shape to the object. You might even arrange your flowers around the object.

Influences

Complementary forms The addition of various objects to an arrangement can underline a mood or visual effect. Depending on the effect you want to achieve, you might use objects which are interesting because of their shape, texture or color, like stones or fabrics.

The viewer's perspective Is it only the top of the arrangement that will be visible or will the sides show too? Should one consider the effect when seen from a distance or only close up? Arrangements intended to be admired at close quarters have different design constraints from those intended to be viewed at a distance. In the former case you should highlight an interesting detail: for instance, the contrast formed by the differences in texture of smooth rose hips, rough horse-chestnut cases and velvety soft petals. It would also be possible to place flowers in a deep vase which would be lost at a distance.

Will one side of the arrangement be visible at an angle, as in the case of a dining table arrangement? If so, step back occasionally while arranging your flowers, to see them from the relevant angle. If flowers are intended to be viewed mainly from a distance, it makes sense to use larger shapes and brighter colors. This also applies to arrangements for areas which are often spacious but only passed through, like hallways and stair wells.

The degree of light How will the light change during the day? Will daylight and artificial light alter the color of your flowers? Will artificial light produce an interesting play of shadows on the wall? These changes are fascinating to observe – colors predominating in the middle of the day and shapes in the evening. Always try to do the arrangement where it is to stand, as certain color medleys can look soft and warm in the room where they are arranged but disappointingly dull in their intended location.

What makes an arrangement harmonious? Reactions like, "It gets on my nerves" or "It's boring," which express the opposite of tranquility or movement, mean that the components of the arrangement do not harmonize. It is important to achieve the right balance between these feelings. Artistic designs reflect an important aspect of our lives – adding to the balance between rest and activity, sleep and wakefulness – the lack of which leaves us edgy and restless.

We merely glance at some flower arrangements because they are very ordinary. Others overwhelm us. The aim should be to create a balanced harmony between shapes, colors and textures, through the way in which different flowers are grouped together and through the overall composition of the arrangement.

Some flowers are tranquil and sturdy in character – others are sparkling, slender blooms. Factors which contribute to this include: outline; direction of movement; texture of petal, leaf and stem; size of flower; thickness of stem in relation to flower; construction; fragrance; variety and intensity of color.

Normally we are unaware of these individual details but we are conscious of the whole – the overall effect of a particular plant (see center column). The features of a flower produce individual effects. An overall impression of shape is almost always the dominant factor, while other details influence the effect to a greater or lesser degree. The "shouting" trumpet of the daffodil gives the impression of

Harmony

Shape and movement

Individual shapes

For a tranquil effect:
- unbroken outlines
- round shaped leaves
- straight stems
- minimal number of colors
- matt textures
- large shapes

For a lively effect:
- irregular outlines
- elongated blooms
- curving stems
- flowers with foliage
- a variety of colors
- glossy textures
- various shapes

greater animation than, for instance, the incurved flower head of the tulip. A single-colored tulip seems more tranquil than a multicolored one. A flower with an unbroken outline appears more static than one that is indented. A large-leafed flower appears less "busy" than one with numerous small leaves.

Certain shapes suggest tranquility, for instance, round flower heads or straight stems. Elongated blooms, that give a triangular effect, or those which point in a number of directions, have a restless feel. This may be heightened by leaf shapes and positions and is seen in such flowers as irises, floribunda roses, lilies and larkspur. The impact of a straight-stemmed flower with an elongated flower head, like an iris, can be heightened by the way in which the stem is placed in the arrangement – even though the stem itself is a static element. However, flowers which bend over enhance the feeling of movement. In order to create the right effect, the appropriate flowers should not be cut too short, so their natural character is maintained. A snapdragon for example, which has been cut too close to the flower head, looks cropped and distinctly odd. It is acceptable, however, to cut some flower stems short in order to draw attention to the flower head – as in the case of a fully opened lily – in order to show off the detail of color and texture. On the other hand, an iris in bud, cut down short, loses its character and movement.

What I have said above applies equally to foliage, but experience will soon tell you if you are going wrong.

Certain flowers, for example cosmos, appear to give the effect of movement because of the transparent nature of their petals and their pliant stems. In using such variable shapes as these you must decide, in each individual case, how short to cut the stem. (See page 53).

The natural direction in which a stem or flower bends often provides a clue to how it should be best positioned in an arrangement so that it looks right. Flowers and leaves continuously turn toward the light. It is interesting to notice the change when a flower is placed away from the light. Does it need space to turn a certain way? If so, which way? Will giving the flower head just enough space to turn suffice? Which way does the flower face when it is cut?

Direction of movement

Try drawing the outlines of an anemone and a freesia. You will find that the anemone is very easy to draw because of its apparently symmetrical petals. The shape is easy to remember because of its simple construction. The freesia is another matter. A number of different flower heads, at staggered intervals, cross over each other. Analyzing the shape and form of these takes some time. It makes sense to have an understanding of these details when using such flowers in an arrangement. For instance, I would never place a different species of flower directly adjacent to a freesia in an arrangement, and particularly not one of a similar structure, as nothing should distract from its distinctive outline. A group of freesias can also be used to reflect the shape of a single flower in an arrangement.

Outlines

Flowers with round outlines permit tighter grouping together. Marguerites and daisies, which grow in clumps, ask to be picked. The same feeling is produced by hyacinths and violets. These flowers look delightful displayed simply in a vase in bunches, or singly, with a little greenery.

Imported flowers, like proteas from South Africa and orchids from the Far East, which are relatively expensive, are also very attractive to us, as our native flowers might be abroad, but our own familiar flowers can also be an inspiration. Looking at an entire horse chestnut tree we are aware of the color and splendor. Examining a single twig carefully we become aware of the contrast between its bent, dark, roughness and the delicate, colorful, tiny, symmetrically placed flower heads which make up each candle. Looking at individual blossoms we see the interesting outline of the petals and the colors. Detailed examination is essential to be aware of these points and we should try not to let the sheer volume of detail distract us.

Getting it right

Up to this point we have dealt with the effect a single flower has on us. But a number of the points discussed earlier (summarized in the middle column of pages 21 and 23) apply equally to the arrangement as a whole. Generally speaking, the choice of flowers, design of the arrangement and intended effect should all interact. The arrangement as a whole may be lively or tranquil, as is the case with a single flower.

By using flowers with stems of the same length, you draw the attention to color and texture. If, however, flowers vary in height, it is the outline shapes that are highlighted. A symmetrical outline to an arrangement can underline the tranquil effect of the flowers, or can act as a contrast when flowers of differing shapes and various colors are used.

To achieve the right balance between tranquility and liveliness in an arrangement, the flowers, design, and method of arranging have to be carefully chosen. An arrangement which seems too "busy" can be calmed down by reducing the size of the outline and the number of different shapes and colors, and by using flowers limited to a single season. There are many ways to make an arrangement look more lively. Consider for moment what it is that you find attractive about a particular arrangement or bunch of flowers? Does it remind you of music or a walk you once took, or give you a feeling of happiness and contentment? Is it exciting and powerful in the way that jazz is or does it remind you of a gentle melody? Does it reflect some aspect of nature? Does it attract you because it is the right design in the right situation?

Then ask yourself what is creating the impression received. Is it due to the variety or the single kind of flower used? Perhaps it is the shape, movement, color and texture of the design? What effect does the outline have on you? The way in which the flowers are arranged within it and the proportion of greenery? Which elements give an impression of tranquility and which of liveliness? All this helps to make us aware of what we should (subconsciously, at any rate) take into account when creating an arrangement. It is extremely important to trust your own instincts – this book can only give you ideas and inspirations. The love of flowers comes from the enjoyment of nature. Doing it "right" is not important. It is right when you like the results and they reflect your own ideas. Experiment at becoming familiar with the characteristics of individual flowers and you will develop the necessary affection for them.

There is one key question I always ask myself and my pupils or clients when designing an arrangement: what is the setting to be?

Are flowers to be of one kind and one color?

If not then you need to take into consideration:
- the season
- color scheme
- visual atmosphere
- plant and container materials and textures
- combination of different shapes
- combination of similar shapes

Consider how the flowers are to be arranged:

- with stems all the same length
- with stems of different lengths
- with flowers of a similar type and color massed together
- or singly

You soon will discover that your own mood or emotions play a role in the way you treat an arrangement: you may handle your flowers in a relaxed manner, arranging them lightly and without a great deal of thought, alternatively, you may work carefully, taking a long time over them, or you may feel inspired to work swiftly. There is no definitive method for flower arranging since no two sets of conditions are ever the same. The choice of flowers, settings and occasion are never precisely repeated. The important thing is to express your own creativity and to let nature influence your work.

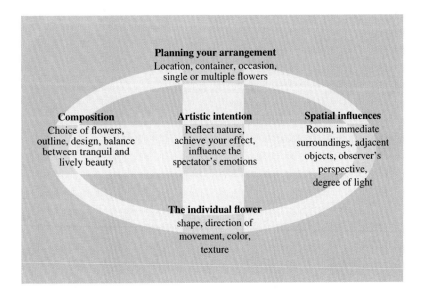

Planning your arrangement
Location, container, occasion, single or multiple flowers

Composition
Choice of flowers, outline, design, balance between tranquil and lively beauty

Artistic intention
Reflect nature, achieve your effect, influence the spectator's emotions

Spatial influences
Room, immediate surroundings, adjacent objects, observer's perspective, degree of light

The individual flower
shape, direction of movement, color, texture

SPRING

There is a moment, as winter ends and daylight grows, when it feels as if nature is at a standstill and everything in the garden and landscape is dormant. Then suddenly spring bursts forth and flowers appear apparently from nowhere – though of course they have been quietly preparing for this moment throughout the winter months. Blossom appears, the first flowers peep out and buds can be seen on shrubs and trees. Gradually the first tender green shoots unfold and plants emerge. At the start of springtime we are still influenced by the colors of winter – white snowdrops, fallen brown leaves and stark branches, but as the new season expands, the world becomes ever more colorful – until at last the delightful messengers of spring herald the end of winter.

Composition in parallel

Against the still predominant browns of the
tree branches, the light, fresh colors of the
first leaves, the fresh green larch, the sloe
blossoms and brilliant ranunculus (from a
florist), seem to breathe spring. The twigs,
which all curve in one direction, contrast
visually with the thicker upright branches,
the wide bands used to secure the
arrangement and the pottery dish. Sawed-
off branches are first tied together to form
a secure structure, flowers and blossom are
then tied to them and the arrangement is
self-supporting in water without any
further securing.

Arrangement with Christmas roses

A wintry feel to this – suitable for the
period just after Christmas. The variety of
foliage of different origins is highlighted
by the inclusion of more homely sprigs and
by the sparing use of Christmas roses. The
color scheme and symmetrical outline
emphasize the shapes and textures of
flowers and foliage. This arrangement will
keep for a long time, as it dries out only
gradually and individual items can be
replaced. Position the upright stems first, in
wet floral foam, followed by the horizontal
and, lastly, the diagonal items. Christmas
roses do not last long in floral foam so
their stems should be placed directly in the
water, supported by foliage.

Golden springtime

A simple, well defined arrangement is created here by the use of a single color and a single type of flower, tightly packed. This treatment highlights the shape, color and texture of the tulip flower heads and the overall arrangement creates interesting effects of light and shade. Over a few days the tulips will begin to open out and their outlines gradually break up. If you wish to delay this, cut them shorter each day.

Spring table decorations

This wreath is both easy to arrange and is long lasting. The ring is formed by binding vine or other creeper stems together. Flowers of varying lengths are placed in the ring at such an angle that their stems reach the water. Artificial or dried flowers can be used instead of fresh ones. Arranged with suitable materials, the ring can also be used as a door wreath (add a string tie) and as the basis of an Advent wreath by including conifer foliage, wired cones, rose hips, cinnamon sticks, nuts and pieces of ginger (see page 65). With its center covered in moss, to form a nest containing eggs, it also turns into an Easter ring. Rings and wreaths are fun all year round, not just at Christmastime.

Two strands of vine or creeper stems are twined into a circle and tied at opposite sides. To keep an open effect, take care not to bind them too tightly.

Lay a few more vine strands loosely around the ring and tie in at various points – they must start and end in different places. Now twist a little fine wire around the wreath to hold it together.

The wreath is now ready for greenery to be added. The choice of foliage will depend on the season and the effect you wish to create. Always make sure the ring keeps its semitubular, as well as its circular, shape and, when tying in foliage, attach it only to a couple of points so as not to flatten the ring. Finally, twist another piece of wire round the finished wreath.

Spring table decorations

These typically springlike arrangements are very simple and can be prepared a couple of days before a party. The undersides of the plantpots are covered in foil to protect the tablecloth and the pots are covered in crepe paper, held in place with colored ribbon. Other forms of decorative paper can also be bought in specialist shops.

Individual arrangements of this kind have several advantages. Groups of pots can be interspersed on the table with such items as serving dishes and the condiments – even just a few pots can look attractive. Flower groups can be repeated as often as you wish, making it simple to plan your table for five guests or fifty. For six to eight guests, one five-pot group would be sufficient. It is important that flowers are of varying heights but take care that the tallest does not obstruct anyone's view. African violets and ivy look well with this kind of treatment and there is a wide variety of seasonal plants that would be suitable. In addition to positioning your pots you might also lay wide, colored ribbon down the center of the table to link your pots together. If only a few guests are expected, small bunches of flowers on the napkins can look very attractive.

Planted spring basket

This arrangement will continue to look attractive for months, positioned in good light in a cool hallway or near the front door. The wicker basket appears to cradle the tender spring plants – an effect which is heightened by clematis tendrils. The bottom of the basket is covered with a thick layer of foil, with pebbles and potting compost on top, in which a glass of water is embedded to give the clematis tendrils their own water supply.

The essence of spring

The desiccated browns of winter have disappeared at last and true spring is here. Colorful posies of spring flowers in various sizes are divided between vases of staggered height, possibly with a linking color theme or, as here, randomly. My four-year-old daughter arranged these from the garden – a simple mixture of wild and cultivated flowers. This kind of arrangement can look as good in a formal setting as in a country home.

Design with Iceland poppies

It is the contrasting textures of this arrangement which make it exciting: the smooth matt leaf of the aspidistra; the rough, hairy poppy stems and wrinkled, transparent flower heads, against the glazed surface of the vase. The plant material is fixed by means of a heavy pinholder. This arrangement looks particularly attractive positioned at eye level and visible from all sides.

A bouquet of tulips

A delicious combination of tulips and broom expresses the freshness of spring. The flowers were placed in the vase, starting at the center and working outward. The smooth texture of the tulips is echoed in the glass of the bowls and their bright color is coolly contrasted by the pale coloring of the bowls. On the left stands a bowl in which float hyacinth florets and, on the right, two scilla plants stand in a flower pot within a bowl.

A Birthday tribute

An arrangement, containing the appropriate number of candles, to be lit as it is brought to the table, makes an enchanting surprise! Ensure each candle is positioned so that the flame cannot burn the plant material and any hot wax drops onto the leaves or flowers and not onto the table. To wire candles into an arrangement, twist a support wire firmly around the bottom of the candle. (Please remember never to leave a lighted arrangement unattended).

Shades of green

An arrangement that contains no flowers in bloom can still look extremely attractive. The subtle nuances of different shades of green become apparent, as do the individual patterns and textures. Looked at from above it forms a circle and, from the side, a semicircle. To achieve this outline, the stems of the varying types of foliage must mainly be cut to the same length, though tight, flat forms will need to be cut a little shorter than slender, narrow ones. (See technique for tying bunches on page 15).

Green bouquet with tulips

This arrangement needs only a few flowers, dotted evenly throughout, to give a rich effect but the same number of tulips, with only a little foliage, would look rather meager. On the other hand, this size and style of arrangement using a large quantity of tulips but with only a few sprigs of foliage would look very unattractive.

Shades of pink

The effect of this arrangement depends on using varying shades of pink. Here, other varieties of pink flowers are used, in addition to tulips. Make sure that all flower stems bend in the same direction and do not cross each other. Foliage no longer plays the dominant role in this variation but is still an important factor in terms of pattern and texture.

Glowing colors

This variation is strikingly cheerful and evocative of spring. The symmetrical outline acts as a stabilizing and tranquil factor in an otherwise riotously colorful arrangement. The largest flowers, in this case tulips, form the main feature and you may find that a certain amount of experimentation is required to create this look successfully. It can be arranged as a whole but it is much easier if the basic

SUMMER

Summer is a time of abundance and color in the garden. The blaze of poppy and cornflower, punctuated by the white marguerite and, later in the season, the creamy gold of ornamental grasses, irresistibly spell summer. Early in the season, clear, sparkling colors dominate; in high summer come the warm, diffuse shades of yellow and in late summer we have the deep, rich shades of orange and the ripening fruits which announce the onset of autumn.

Scents, too, are rich and fragrant in summer. This is the time when I like to wander through my garden and pick a few sprigs of green or flowering shrubs and herbs: lavender, mint, lemon balm, sage, and those wild herbs which are to be found everywhere at this season. A handful of roses; a little yarrow; some nasturtiums; zinnias, and camomile also find their way into my hands. The rich effect of summer is easy to achieve now.

Horse-chestnut "candles"

The candle shaped flowers of the horse-chestnut tree always grow upward, toward the light. Placed, as in this arrangement – stripped of leaves and upside down – the effect is striking.

The bareness and simplicity of the composition permit every detail of the blossom to be seen. The proportions of the glass vase – tall and narrow – and of the short bending twigs, are also unusual. If you follow the curve of the flowering area of the composition with your eyes, you understand how important the height of the vase and the depth of space below the flower heads are to the drama of the arrangement as a whole.

Early summer table decoration

This is an elegant design, suitable for important occasions, though it is informal and relaxed in its composition. The tendrils form a visual link between the flower containers and might even swirl around the place setting for the guest of honor. This table design is most effective when flat plates are used.

A block of well-soaked floral foam is cut into a half circle and covered with flat greenery and small flowers. Longer sprigs of foliage and flowers are arranged in the foam so that they all curve in one direction. This arrangement requires flowers and foliage which naturally bend or can be easily shaped.

Flowering broom and butcher's broom are supplemented by vine tendrils. Leaves and flowers are then attached to colored wire at suitable intervals, which is then trailed informally across the table. You need to experiment to see which leaves and flowers last longest out of water.

Summer basket

The basket used is the same as for the arrangement below – but to completely different effect. Here the hot blaze of summer color is the dominant note. The arrangement is intended to look as though the flowers are lying in the basket as if just gathered from the garden. A few sprigs of greenery draw the composition together visually. Since the flowers used here are larger and more compact than those used below, they have to be cut shorter.

Meadow basket

Wild flowers are the theme here in this gently hazy, early summer arrangement. But a noble, yellow peony, positioned on the right near the handle of the basket, and the large horse-chestnut blossom on the left, form unusual counterpoints to this, otherwise, very open arrangement. The dark color and solid shape of the basket also emphasize the delicate structures of the plant material.

Moss-covered container with lily

In contrast to the blaze of summer color in the arrangement below, this lily composition in its moss-covered container strikes a cool note. The foliage echoes the pattern of the lily petals and the vulnerable tendrils of pink flowering wild vetch form a delightful contrast. Textures of leaf and flower are emphasized: from rough (the texture of moss), to matt, to velvet and shining gloss. The coppery color of the wire which binds the container is repeated in the gold and copper-stamened lily. The areas of color on the left of the composition counterbalance the larger leaves on the right: silver, yellow and pink draw the eye across. The size and weight of this arrangement mean it is best positioned to be viewed from the side. Since the opening of the container used is very narrow no foam is required, as the plant material will be self-supporting.

Summer riches

Redolent of the height of summer, in all its lush, rich blaze of color, this arrangement uses both wild and garden flowers. Here a number of tied bunches of small flowers are used. Either wire mesh, crushed into a ball, or floral foam may be used as fixings. Care must be taken that a composition so tightly packed does not end up looking squashed. Flat shaped, small flowers can be arranged so they partially overlap each other. A few flowers break out of the solid whole and remove any feeling of stiffness. The composition gradually loosens up to the left-hand side but is still tight enough for it to be flower heads, rather than stems, that are emphasized. Flowers of all kinds mix happily together; the aristocratic rose with the humble wild flower, herbaceous perennials, geranium and flowering clover. An arrangement of this kind can be built up from individual posies throughout the summer or by replacing individual flowers as they fade. It lasts well as the flowers are placed close together and cut very short but check the water level regularly.

Terracotta planter arrangement

A delightfully random arrangement planted in a
terracotta container. The trailing plants run
riotously over each other in a tangle of color
and movement. This needs to be replanted
every year, though some plants will keep over
winter. An attractive variation is to let trailing
plants hang down round most sides of the pot,
like a decorative shawl, but it is important to
use small plants at the front and back. Pebbles
in the bottom of the pot serve as a water
reservoir. Plants which are packed so tightly
together will need feeding from time to time, to
keep them going from spring, through the
summer growing season, to autumn.

Garden grace

A particularly rich and delightful effect
can be achieved by mixing garden
flowers and wild flowers. To create this
graceful effect, simply place naturally
drooping or trailing flowers at the outer
edges of the arrangement. A few longer
sprays are placed on top to curve over.

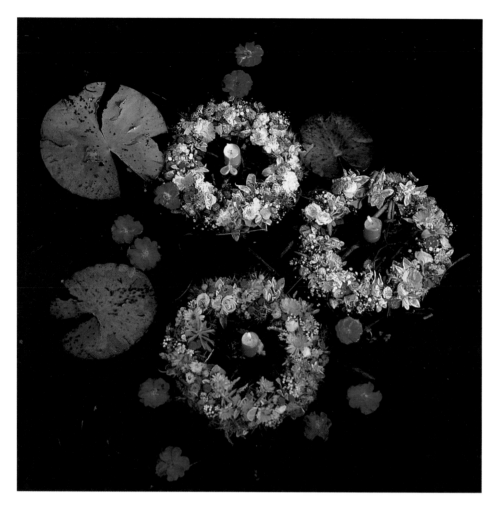

Floating flower rings

This is a revival of an old summer solstice tradition. Small wreaths of flowers and leaves, with candles in the center, float on a small garden pond or water basin. On a windless summer evening they look extremely romantic. They may also be placed in bowls of water for longer lasting enjoyment.

Wooden cross pieces are wired to a narrow hoop. A cushion of moss is then wired to the center and small flowers and foliage wired round the hoop. Lastly, a candle is fixed into the moss by means of a wire twisted around its base and then attached firmly to the structure .

44

Summer table arrangement

A simple summery arrangement that is suitable for a party in the garden. Very short cut flowers are bunched tightly together on a plate. Ivy is entwined around them and trailed the length of the table – outdoor varieties will survive without water at least for as long as the party lasts. Other fragile looking trailing plants may be used in this arrangement, which is also suitable for long tables, with the ivy trails linking each flower plate.

Decorative ball

An unusual little gift to take your hostess for a beach or riverside party. The blue of the glass ball and the sand in which it is sitting echo the blue of the water and the sandy beach. A pleasantly cool arrangement which will need to be replanted or repotted after the party, as the plants will not survive if left too long in wet sand.

Impressions of summer

Shades of yellow, orange and red set the tone of this design. The white of the container is echoed in the shells while the green of the geranium leaf and trailing vetch punctuate the whole when placed accurately. Shells are also used to hold the flowers.

1

3

2

4

Late summer arrangement

1. Place a block of soaked floral foam in the container, ensuring it rises above the rim to accommodate side flowers. Flowers will need to be of varying lengths according to the design you wish to create. Start from the outer edges of the composition, placing the vertical and horizontal pieces in position first. Colors will need to be mixed to create a riotous but well-balanced composition.

2. Having positioned the main feature, the roses, and decided on the outline, additional flowers may now be added, taking care not to detract from the main feature. In this arrangement various soft, lacy effect herbs, wild strawberries and hops were used.

3. At this point a few yellow roses and other yellow flowers are arranged in the gaps to provide color contrast. To achieve a natural looking effect, colors should be mixed and distributed fairly randomly throughout the composition. To lighten the arrangement, a few white and pink roses are included.

4. Even this illustration seems fragrant with the scent of roses and herbs. These flowers, in their warm, muted shades, are redolent of late summer. Take care that bright colors and sharply defined shapes are surrounded by small flowered, discreet plants and that wild flowers neighbor the more sophisticated rose.

Foaming plenty

Large bunches of summer flowers are simply grouped
together in a rustic container. Bunches of individual
varieties are tied up beforehand and the stems cut. Start
your arrangement by working from the outside in. The
main areas of pattern are provided by the large shining
flowers of the Peruvian lily, the white marguerites, and the
green and white euphorbias. Light mauve adds a touch of
complementary color.

AUTUMN

Rich colors, rounded forms and a variety of berries are the
keynote of autumn, as nature begins to retreat into
reflection. As we watch the pale leaves fall from the trees
we begin to feel nostalgic for the blazing colors of
summer. And, as the cold, bareness of approaching winter
begins to creep up on us, the rich reds and golds of
autumn are doubly welcome in our flower arrangements.
This is the time when I start a collection. Like a squirrel
I hoard supplies: rose hips, sweet chestnut cases, horse
chestnuts, hop and other vine tendrils – particularly those
which can be dried and used right through to springtime.

At times, close, detailed observation of a flower is the best way to describe it. The cosmos is one of the few flowers which bloom from late summer until the first frosts of autumn. While in tropical and sub-tropical areas of the Americas they grow wild.

The flowers appear tender and fragile and reminiscent of a butterfly, alighting gently. The petal structure is simple and appears almost transparent, particularly in the case of white cosmos. The frayed leaf outline is a characteristic of the plant and its appearance of vulnerability is highlighted by the delicate leaves and gently bending stem. If you touch the stem, bud, leaf or flower of a cosmos you will find the stems are rough textured, the buds moist and smooth, and the flowers velvety soft. But, despite its appearance to the contrary, cosmos are in fact hardy, abundantly flowering garden plants.

Arranging flowers singly which normally grow in clumps, can be fun. The following six arrangements are on varying principles and the cosmos is used both on its own and with other flowers. Sometimes they form the main feature in the composition and sometimes they are simply an element. If you wish to emphasize the seasonal impression of the cosmos or a physical feature, like its transparency and form, you can do so either by arranging numbers of the same flower or by including flowers which contrast with them. The transparency and texture of a glass vase echo the attributes of cosmos petals, while the addition of rough textured or dried plant material will highlight their softness and freshness.

Cosmos with berries

The heavy feeling of solidity, created by the compactness of the bowl and weight of the berries, is balanced by the effect of fragile, slender-stemmed cosmos which are left long. The glass bowl echoes the color and texture of the flower petals. In its clarity and coolness this arrangement elegantly expresses a feeling of approaching autumn.

50

All in white

Here is a composition that, in its soft fullness, is still reminiscent of summer. The creamy shades of the flowers, used in addition to the cosmos, highlight its elegance. Even though the arrangement displays a number of patterns and textures, the outline produces an effect of tranquility, with berries neighboring vine tendrils, and matt and velvety smooth textures juxtaposed. The different shades of cream and white create a play of light and shade, deepened by touches of creamy yellow, green and pale green.

Autumn vines with cosmos

The dominant theme in this arrangement is autumn itself, in all its charm. The cosmos here is just a detail in the composition – though an important one. The rough texture of the container is echoed by that of the vine root, from whose hollows issue berries, fruit, leaves, flowers and vine tendrils. Rough and coarse textures and forms here act as a contrast to the much softer, lighter plant material.

A bright bouquet with cosmos

The last flowers of summer and the first flowers of autumn work together here. This arrangement is characterized by a rich variety of patterns, shapes and colors. The cosmos, without being dominant, contributes beautifully and the fragrant composition is airy and natural looking. Tendrils and shoots add a playful note to this farewell to summer and show it is not all sadness.

Cosmos contrasted with twigs

The brown and black background formed by container and cut twigs makes a strong contrast to the white shades of the cosmos. The rough textures also highlight the softness of the flower, while the twigs, plastic tubing and grass draw lines to tie the composition together. The bundle of twigs also acts as a foundation to hold the flower stems. Make sure the ends of the stems are well down in the water.

Cosmos composition

The intention of this composition is to emphasize – in a completely new way – the lightness and transparency which characterize cosmos. A number of flower holders, each containing a single flower, are arranged in a linear composition. Two are silver, one is yellow and these provide the element of color. Russian vine tendrils underline, in a playful manner, the design effect of the cosmos. Crossed stems and flowers that face each other, draw the whole composition together.

Simply carnations

This arrangement shows a stunningly
different way to present such an everyday
flower as the carnation. Unusually, colors
are mixed and flowers packed tightly
together, instead of being loosely arranged.
People who normally find carnations
ordinary will see these through different
eyes. The use of a glass vase allows the
observer to see the pattern formed by the
stems and the container itself becomes a
showcase. The angled rim of the vase is
gently echoed in the solid outline of the
flower heads.

Impressions of late autumn

The inspiration for this arrangement was a fallen branch with a few dried leaves from the previous year still hanging on and contrasting interestingly with the green leaves and tiny white blossoms that appear on it. The bush from which it came was shaped like a sheltering umbrella and this is echoed in the outline and composition of the arrangement. Spray chrysanthemums of varying shades are arranged so that only blocks of color, rather than individual flowers, vary in height, to add an element of tranquility.

Impressions of early autumn

A blend of warm, bright and muted colors characterize this arrangement. By using a container with a wide opening there are various design options available. Here, two strong branches are wedged in to give additional support to the plant materials. The flowers are positioned vertically and mixed with seasonal fruit and foliage. A branch of maple, some sunflowers, ivy and Chinese lanterns are used here.

Autumn country bowl

Australian wild flowers, a few larger yellow proteas from a specialist shop, summer cypress, statice, and dried oak leaves give this arrangement its rustic, hardy look. All these flowers can be dried by giving them less water after a couple of weeks and then stopping it altogether. The overseas plant materials are not cheap but will last a long time. Keep the arrangement compact to give a sturdy, robust effect matching the characteristics of the plant material. If you want to make a similar design using plant material from your garden, select flower heads which dry well.

Red roses

This is a glorious wedding day arrangement. To emphasize the bridal element, white gypsophila is used and loosely tied white tulle ribbons. The rose-printed gold ribbon adds a distinctive touch and is also used for the big bow tied round the pot to link both arrangement and container. The roses are arranged in wet floral foam which dispenses with the need for supporting foliage and allows each individual rose to be shown to its best advantage. Remember always to buy good quality flowers (see page 14), particularly for such a special occasion.

WINTER

In wintertime I always gaze in wonder at the bare trunks and
branches of trees and at the patterns made by areas of revealed
light and sky framed by the branches which are hidden by
summer foliage. The shapes are curved in the case of the horse
chestnut tree and elongated triangles in the pattern of the lime.
The fragile tracery of birch twigs form the same pattern as the
heavier branches of the alder.

Certain shrubs, like rose bushes or the sloe, keep their
hips and berries for a long while and some right through to
spring. Nature is pleasantly inactive at this time and the feeling
of tranquility is enhanced by muted colors, punctuated by
occasional points of warmer color and by winter's blurred
outlines. I love to express this feeling of peace through the use
of winter tones in my flower compositions and many people
find that such arrangements are the most successful way to
express the atmosphere of this season.

A winter tree

This enchanting and unususal decoration is suitable for the whole season of parties. The glow of light and play of fascinating shadow in the evenings and the pleasure of colors, patterns and textures which this arrangement gives in day time, make it an all round success. The little tree announces that winter is here, reminds us it will soon be Christmas and can continue to be displayed until spring arrives. To recreate this tree every year takes time but is interesting and fun to do. Almost every item of plant material used was gathered and picked by hand.

1. The pattern for this tree is the standard laurel or bay tree with its slender trunk and round topped shape, stripped of its foliage. Take time to construct the head of the tree so that it is sturdy. It is formed from twigs and strong tendrils which are twined into a ball shape and attached to a firm, straight branch which forms the trunk. The branch which represents the trunk is best set in plaster in an earthenware plant pot and then the surface covered with small stones for decoration.

2. A string of fairy lights is then threaded through the ball, ensuring they are arranged symmetrically. Gold ribbon and a quantity of leaves, like holly and conifer, are then anchored round the ball. A variety of materials, including feathers and transparent materials, looks good and should be layered so the lights are invisible but shine through them.

3. Lastly, ribbon is wired to the tree and thin colored string and gold wire twisted all round the ball to give additional support as well as to look decorative.

1

3

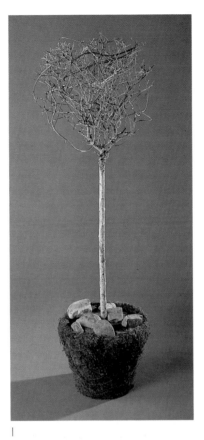

2

Christmas arrangement

Gerberas, greenery and colored ribbon are combined in a
harmonious composition. The friendly little Santa Claus
adds a cheery seasonal note. This arrangement is very
useful in this busy season as the gerberas can be replaced as
they wilt, without having to re-do the whole design. The
greenery will last for several weeks if kept moist. However,
if flowers are beyond your budget at Christmas, just add
more foliage or some small Christmas tree balls on wire
stems. Keep the balls to one color for best effect.

Advent wreath

Various traditional decorations and chubby, old fashioned, marbled candles give a really traditional Christmas effect to this wreath. Tiny red balls, artificial flowers, leaves sprayed gold, thistle heads, baroque angels and scrolls of Christmas paper are simply pinned on at intervals. A single, shining red, reflecting, Christmas tree ball adds a further dimension.

The technique used to make this wreath is so simple that it is fun for children to make. Conifer leaves are stapled flat to the ring of dry foam. Remaining plant materials are stuck into the ring with wire or their own stems.

1

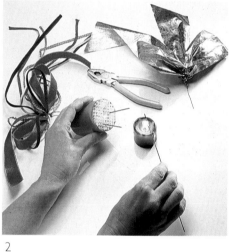

2

3

Bound Advent wreaths

The two wreaths illustrated here are bound wreaths. The larger one is luxuriously decorated with ribbon but a variety of decorations could be used, fir cones and gold-sprayed seed heads with colored cord twisted around. Using a variety of foliage can also be effective – but just enjoy making it up in any materials you have to hand. The small wreath is easy to prepare and would make a lovely gift.

1. Cut foliage into pieces 2–4 inches (5–10 cm) long. Cover a ring base (obtainable in specialist shops or florists) with green paper ribbon or crepe paper cut into strips and twist wire once around it. To secure the wire, push one end of it well into the ring. Place a piece of greenery on the inner side of the ring and stretch wire over. Repeat, working across the section of ring until you reach the outer edge. Now twist the wire round the ring to anchor the foliage in place.

Make sure that the foliage all points in a clockwise direction. When a number of rows have been secured, it may be necessary then to start afresh each time from the center to avoid covering leaf areas with wire, rather than stems. When ring is completely covered, cut the wire and push the end in to secure.
2. The ribbon bows are tied beforehand (see page 12) and secured in the wreath after the foliage is completed. The widest layer of each bow is secured first and the narrower ones fixed on top, in descending order of size. To secure candles, take three pieces of heated wire for each candle and insert into the wax bases. This wire must be strong enough to support the candle when attached.
3. To make the little wreath: wire leftover pieces (about 1.5 inches, 4 cm long) of box and fir onto another piece of wire to form a ring and decorate with small bows and tiny candles.

Entwined Advent wreath

Traditional colors and materials are used in this wreath.
Cinnamon, ginger and nutmeg mingle with sprigs of pine,
nuts, ivy, rose hips and roses. The roses are kept watered by
being placed in moss-covered single stem holders. Use
artificial flowers if this is more convenient. How to make
the basic ring for this wreath is described on page 29. The
wreath should be placed on a decorative base before the
decorations are added as it is otherwise impossible to carry
once finished.

1

3

2

4

Festive table decorations

1. Twist a little thin wire, silver cord or tinsel around a pine twig which has been bent into a curve. Add a decoration.

2. Decorative herbs, spices, rose hips and holly leaves are wired to a twig with very fine wire. This makes a fragrant place, or placecard, decoration.

3. A small poinsettia, with bows and golden stars sprinkled around it, is a quickly made festive decoration.

4. A moss-covered single stem holder ensures this Christmas rose is kept watered.

These ideas can also be used as inspiration for other imaginative decorations, which could double as little gifts for your guests.

Winter "snow"

The color scheme and fragile effect of the plant materials used here echo the coldness of winter. This is arranged in floral foam and to achieve an effect of fullness without quantities of greenery and flowers, some dried flowers were also used. The cyclamen are in stem holders, as they do not last in foam. When they wilt, they can simply be replaced in the same holder.

LIVING WITH FLOWERS

Your ability to arrange flowers in a variety of different ways depends on your knowledge and understanding of both their characteristic and unusual features. Firstly, it is important to recognize the factors that make displaying flowers in your home possible. We have taken a living plant out of its natural habitat and, in doing so, we have changed it. The flower we see in the vase is no longer the untouched flower of nature – though it may look entirely natural. It is essential always to be aware that you are handling living plant material, though cut flowers, whether from your garden or shop bought, are no longer living in the way nature intended. By cutting and arranging flowers in a different environment, like our home, we have interrupted the processes of nature. Awareness of this fact is essential to our sensitive handling and arranging of flowers and foliage.

Spring wreath for the door (*left*)

Welcome party guests with a cheerful wreath. The vine tendril and creeper stem base is made as described on page 29. A few sprigs of box and some artificial broom are firmly anchored into it. The ribbon is twisted round the wreath and the large bow and streamers are wired on last. (The instructions how to wire a bow are on page 12.)

Ivy door wreath (*bottom left*)

This is a very simple door wreath of entwined variegated ivies. Copper colored wire was used to bind a quantity of strong, mature creeper stems, of varying lengths, around a ring base.

Christmas door wreath (*bottom right*)

A traditional Christmas wreath hanging from a decorative cord. A variety of evergreens, gold-sprayed leaves and rose hips are bound on a base (see page 64). The principal features here are the classic Christmas colors and simple decorations.

Door Garland

A special decoration for a special occasion, perhaps a wedding reception at your home. The green garland is composed of three to five long, entwined bean plant or creeper stems, stripped of their leaves and strung together with green wire. Sprigs of asparagus fern and ivy add an aura of richness and help to hide the single stem flower holders which hold summer flowers (see page 13 for how to affix stem holders). The garland may be first hung on the door frame and the flowers then added or the whole may be completed before the garland is hung. It also looks charming with spring flowers, autumn fruit or simply roses. The garland is deliberately left shorter on one side, at the height of the door handle, and this is emphasized by a decorative bow tied from ribbons that pick out the main color of the flowers.

Point of focus

The photographs on the wall and this original arrangement create a decorative point in the room. A warm autumn day is reminiscent of other seasons: the long twigs of winter-flowering Japanese witch hazel stretch beyond the confines of the container, anchored by a heavy stone. Autumn is represented by the bramble, while its blossom reminds us of spring. Toadflax and shepherd's purse tell of summer. The stem ends of the flowers stand in water and are supported by a bundle of bound twigs (see page 52, bottom illustration). The arrangement is sited below eye level so that the combination of photographs and flower arrangement can be seen clearly as a whole composition.

Composition of light and shade

The browny black twigs of sloe were first thinned out, to emphasize the important lines of the composition. The vase, containing the allium flower, is the focal point. The dramatically curving allium stem, counterpoised with the glass ball, is extremely effective and the whole relates to the picture of the outside world, framed by the window.

Autumnal table arrangement

The plant materials, and the height and style of the table, formed the starting point for this design. The table is rather small and is visible from a distant, as well as close up, perspective – which is the reason for using creeper. Graceful, trailing stems, which can dry out, are simply draped over a plant pot. On the righthand side, rose hips create a counter balance. If you wish to include flowers in the pot, cut short the stems on suitable varieties, say, chrysanthemums, so as not to interrupt the freely arching lines of the creeper.

Side table with Advent wreath

The traditional hanging Advent wreath is an evocative decoration. The candles are arranged below it at a safe distance to avoid scorching. Making a hanging wreath of this kind takes time but is worth the effort. Cover the base with a layer of foliage as explained in figure 1 on page 64, then insert pieces of holly, rose hips, box, and ivy and secure firmly. Take care to use evergreens which do not shed their needles when they dry out.

Still life with pottery

Here the "wing" vase is the principal feature of the composition. A gently bending stem bearing rose hips was chosen to echo and lead the eye to the shape of the container. Absolute clarity and minimal use of shapes and colors give this arrangement its charm.

Decoration for a window

A window arrangement which is both colorful and interesting to do. The plastic tubing, bound together, forms the framework and the sparing use of the dried flowers emphasizes their individual detail. This arrangement would also be suitable for a wall but, placed in front of a window, it is particularly eye catching.

Green plant composition

It is always fun to find new ways to display your houseplants. The plants used here remind me of dry earth and sun. The purpose of the arrangement is to highlight the effect that plants can have on each other. The charm of this composition lies in the trailing tendrils which intertwine and form a visual connection between the different shapes. The effect is strengthened by pots being placed behind each other, so that the leaves of the more upright plants also criss-cross.

Design for a windowsill

The beautiful flowering plant is the principal point of this evocative composition. The papery texture of the purple bougainvillea is echoed in the bowl of potpourri in which fragrant, dried flower petals are mixed with dried lavender.

The scent can be revitalised by sprinkling on a little lavender oil from time to time. Like the bougainvillea, the grapes and scent of lavender are reminiscent of the Mediterranean. The shining texture of glass, container and silver pheasants against the folds of the material, form a delightful contrast to the texture of the plant, and the windowsill has become a stage for the composition.

Cool but dramatic

Stephanotis and passion flower swirl round a large planter. As the last of the stephanotis comes into flower, the passion flowers are in full bloom. But the contrasting foliage in this arrangement ensures that interest remains when flowering is over.

Viewed from above, the pattern formed by plants and shells can be seen. This is an unusual but attractive way to use a large plant pot.

If plants are to be planted directly in the pot, it is important that water is stored. This is achieved by creating a drainage system, consisting of a layer of pebbles or broken pieces of clay pot, which will serve as reservoirs.

Roses in the bathroom

This bathroom arrangement has an early autumn charm. On the right of the sill, a tall stem of rose hips, stripped of leaves, echoes the shape of the window and the vine arch framed in it. The rose hip stems, which should dry out slowly, are placed in a tall container – a piece of narrow drainpipe covered with wallpaper would be fun to improvise. The straight-stemmed roses are fixed in floral foam (the shape of the cup container) covered in sand, their tight arrangement forming a counter balance to the graceful branch of hips. Old-fashioned jugs and basins also make decorative containers.

Water plants in a bathroom setting

Vacations at the beach may be over for the year but this composition will be an unusual souvenir. A container is filled with fine sand, followed by large pebbles, shells and marbles. Varying sizes of water plants, with dainty and large leaves are then put in. The container is now filled with water – very carefully, so it does not cloud. A few pond plants are placed on top to keep the water clear. This arrangement does not last for a long time but can still be enjoyed for several months.

PLANT NAMES

The author does not claim that the above list
is complete.

Photography: TLC Foto-Studio GmbH,
Velen Ramsdorf. Illustrations: Ulrike
Hoffmann, Bodenheim. Photographs in top
illustration on page 72 by Fritz Kissels.
Pottery vase in top illustration on page 74
by Karin Utta Altena.

Original German-language edition © 1991
by Falken Verlag GmbH, BLUMEN
LIEBEVOLL ARRANGIEREN
English-language edition © 1995
Transedition Books, a division of
Andromeda Oxford Ltd

This edition published in 1995 by
Transedition Books, a division of Andromeda
Oxford Limited, 11–15 The Vineyard,
Abingdon, Oxfordshire OX14 3PX

This edition printed for
Bookmart Ltd

Printed in 1995 in Spain
by Fournier A. Gráficas, S.A.

ISBN 1 898250 55 3